OCEAN

130°

120°

ARCTIC

CIRCLE

on
City

Mackenzie

DOMINION

DAWSON

Stewart R.

Fort Selkirk

River

OF

60°

Pelly R.

White Horse

Caribou

W. P. & Y.

Bennett

Atlin City

CANADA

R.

Peace

A

SKAGUAY

Juneau

Wrangel

Vancouver

Fraser

River

SITKA

C. P.

50°

O C E A N

Victoria

G.

U.S.

N.

Seattle

Tacoma

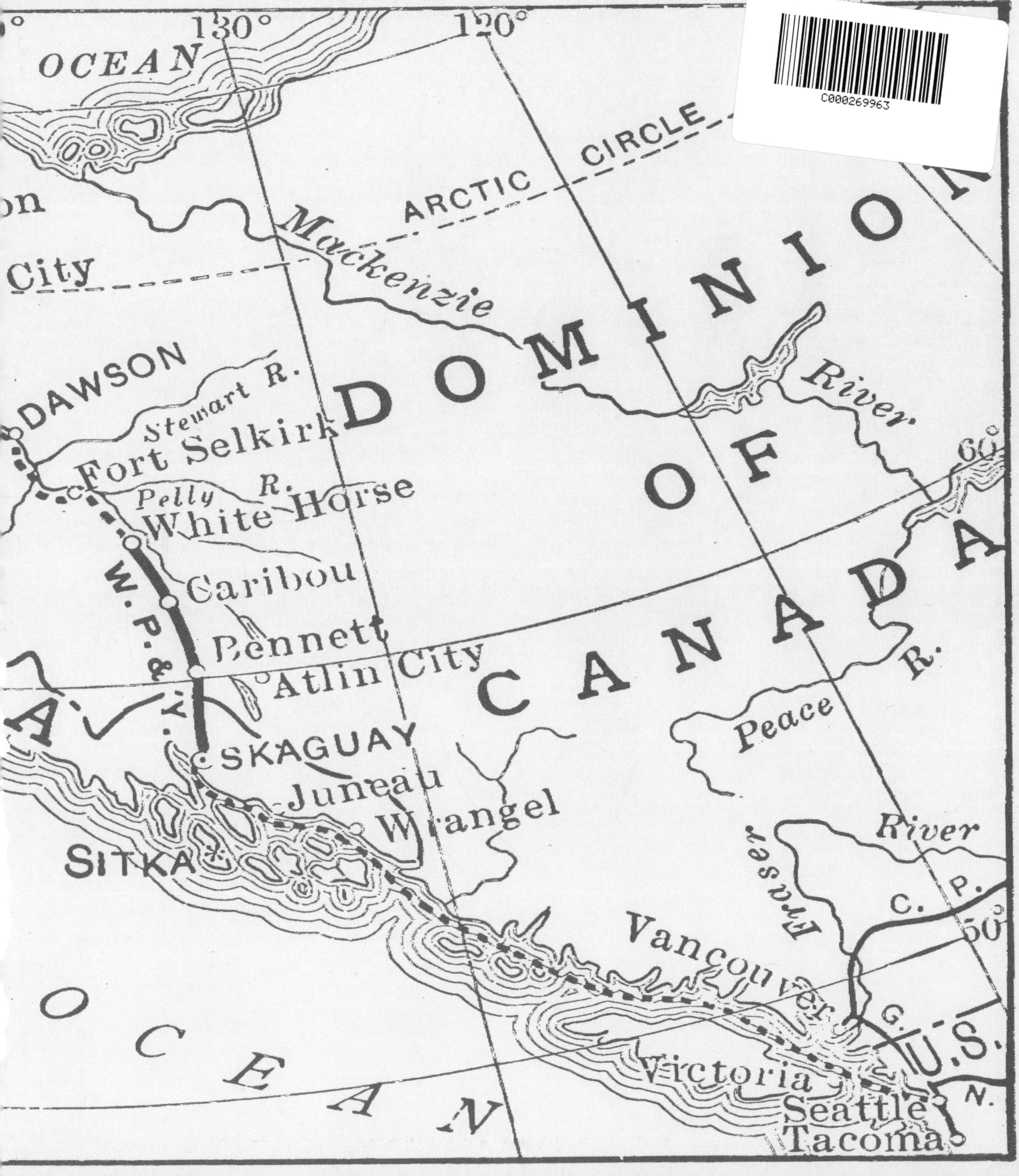

The Illustrated
Robert Service

Todd Communications

Anchorage, Ketchikan, Juneau, Fairbanks and Nome, Alaska

The Illustrated *Robert Service*

Todd Communications
611 E. 12th Avenue, Suite 102
Anchorage, Alaska 99501-4603 U.S.A.
Telephone: (907) 274-TODD (8633)
Telefax: (907) 276-6858
Sales@toddcom.com
WWW.ALASKABOOKSANDCALENDARS.COM

with other offices and warehouses in: Ketchikan, Juneau, Fairbanks & Nome, Alaska

EDITOR, PHOTO RESEARCH AND BOOK DESIGN:
Kathy Doogan/Raven Design & Cartography

First Printing December 2006

10 9 8 7 6 5 4 3 2 1

Library of Congress Control Number: 2006908240

ISBN: 978-1-57833-357-8

Additional copies of this book may be ordered directly from the
publisher for US$19.95 each plus US$6 postage and handling.

Printed in Nansha, China, by Everbest Printing Co., Ltd.

PREVIOUS PAGE: Robert Service, about 1905. (Library & Archives Canada, PA-110158)

Contents

Robert Service on the steps of his cabin in Dawson City, around
1910. Service loved the cabin, noting in his memoir, "Its moose
horns over the porch were like arms stretched out to me."
(Yukon Archives, Martha Louise Black Fonds, #3288)

The Bard of the Yukon

In mid-summer of 1897, word reached the outside world of George Carmacks' discovery of gold on Bonanza Creek near Dawson City, Yukon Territory. A frenzied rush to the area began and thousands of gold-seekers poured into the Klondike, certain they would find their fortune.

It was a search for fortune of another kind that lured Robert Service north.

Service was born January 16, 1874, in Preston, England. At age four he moved with his family to Glasgow, where he attended school until 1888. He dropped out and went to work, first in a shipping office and then as an apprentice for the Commercial Bank of Scotland. By 1895 Service was working as a qualified bank clerk, but was growing increasingly weary of the work, which had never captured his interest. His dream was to go into cattle ranching — what he called the "romantic side of farming" — and he chose Canada as his land of opportunity.

A promotion and a raise, followed by more than a year of penny-pinching, provided Service with the capital needed to follow his dream, and at the age of 22 he quit the bank and booked passage to Canada. He eventually made his way to British Columbia, where he worked on several farms, and then went on to Seattle and San Francisco. He fell in love with the City, spending a month living frugally and getting to know it well. But dwindling funds forced him to look for work. He moved on, finding jobs in Los Angeles and then San Diego, where he was hired as gardener and handyman at an upscale brothel.

Service then took off on the "gipsy trail," starting with a trek around Baja California. A lover of the outdoors and an avid walker who took great pride in his physical fitness, he spent the next two years wandering through the Southwest, working when he needed to, and getting by on $5 a month.

He eventually made his way back to British Columbia, where he worked on a farm in the Cowichan Valley on Vancouver Island. He left the farm in May 1903 with $200 he had saved, and a new goal — to get a university degree and become a teacher. He spent months studying for the entrance examination, and, although barely passing, gained admittance. But he soon realized that he felt "stupid and out of place" and, at age 29, was unable to compete with the younger students' minds. With a great sense of relief, Service gave up on higher education and turned his attention to finding a way to make something of his life.

Down and out in Vancouver, Service reluctantly turned to his bank training and in October 1903 found a job with the Canadian Bank of Commerce in its Victoria branch. In November he was offered a transfer to the branch in Whitehorse, Yukon Territory. The job was considered a prize; not only was the salary higher, but workers in Whitehorse received a $200 cold-weather clothing allowance, an additional $50 per month to help offset the high cost of food, and were provided free lodging. Service set out for the North with the thought that he was beginning a "new and wonderful chapter" in his life.

Enjoying the scenic, all-expenses-paid trip through the Inside Passage, Service thought how nice it would be to always live at the expense of others. So he devised a plan he called his "escape idea." He would save enough money to live off the earnings, occasionally supplementing his income by writing. Since he had always been able to live modestly, he figured $5,000 would be adequate; at five percent interest, this sum would give him about $20 per month to live on.

Service arrived in Whitehorse in November 1904, excited to be beginning what he later called one of the happiest periods of his life. He quickly settled into his new life, relishing the winter, when business at the bank was slow and he could don his snowshoes and take long walks into the wilderness surrounding the town.

Service also embraced the bustling social life in Whitehorse. "I do not believe as small a community has ever packed so much pleasure into its leisure," he wrote in his memoir, *Ploughman of the Moon*. There was hockey and tennis, swimming in summer, dinner parties, dances and theatricals. Service's forte was recitation, and he often fell back on old standards such as "Casey at the Bat" and "Gunga Din." As these selections became more repetitive, friends encouraged him to write something original. The result was "The Shooting of Dan McGrew," a piece that came so easily he claimed it was as if "someone was whispering in my ear."

The poem went into a drawer for several months, then a story related at a dinner party inspired Service to write "The Cremation of Sam McGee." By late 1906 he had completed 34 poems and decided to have them made into a small book to give as Christmas gifts. The publisher he sent them to recognized their potential, and offered to publish the poems commercially. Service happily agreed, and the resulting book, *Songs of A Sourdough* (later published

in the United States as *The Spell of the Yukon*), became an instant success. The unassuming bank clerk was suddenly on his way to wealth and fame.

In late 1907, Service traveled back to Vancouver on a three-month paid vacation, then was reassigned in April 1908 to the bank branch in Dawson City.

As much as he liked being back in the Yukon, Service increasingly disliked his job. His responsibility for large amounts of money and fear of making a mistake caused him much anxiety. As he became more determined to step up his efforts to attain financial freedom, royalties for *Songs of A Sourdough* began to arrive. With these royalties amounting to more than four times his bank salary, Service quickly reached his $5,000 goal, only to increase it to $10,000, an amount he said would put him "in a spot where I could thumb my nose at the world."

Thus motivated, he set about writing his second volume of verse. He was a good listener, and took every opportunity to talk with those who had experienced the gold rush first hand, storing up tales he would craft into poems. Using this material, he worked doggedly on the book, waking himself each night to write during the quiet hours of midnight to 3:00 a.m. *Ballads of A Cheechako*, a collection of 21 poems, was completed in four months.

He expected the book, which he had found difficult to write, to be a failure. But it succeeded, he later wrote, because "...it was sheerly of the North. It was steeped in the spirit of the Klondike. It was written on the spot and reeking with reality."

With royalties coming in on two books, Service found that he could sit back and take life easy. He

Robert Service and his daughter, Iris, on a Brittany beach near Dream Haven, early 1920s. (Yukon Archives, Gillis Family Fonds, #4538)

continued working at the bank, but did no more writing for two years, instead spending his free time walking the trails around Dawson or occupying himself with snowshoe parties, sleigh rides, dances and other social activities. One Sunday, while on a fishing trip up the Klondike River, he came up with the idea of writing a novel about the gold rush, to recreate a past "that otherwise would be lost forever."

Once winter set in Service tried to settle down to write, but found he needed seclusion to let his imagination work and allow him to put words on paper. Then he was told he had been promoted to manager of the Whitehorse branch of the bank. The added responsibilities of being manager and the thought of leaving Dawson, the setting for his novel, helped him decide to quit his job and devote his time to writing. Reassured by a bank balance of just over $10,000, he left his job in November 1909 and moved into a two-room log cabin high on the hillside above town, commenting "the view was inspiring, the isolation all I could have wished."

After completing the final version of *The Trail of '98, A Northland Romance* in April 1910, he decided to make his first trip Outside in five years, to deliver the manuscript himself to his New York publisher.

Service did not enjoy his time in New York. He said the city intimidated him and the literary crowd snubbed him, acting superior and patronizing. His book was a success, but soon he once again heard the call of the "gipsy trail."

This time the trail took him south, first to New Orleans then on to Havana, where he remained until fall, when the heat turned his thoughts to the "snow and tonic air of the North."

He decided to head to Alberta to visit his mother, who he had not seen in 13 years. He remained on the family farm through the winter, helping with chores, taking long hikes on the vast prairie and getting to know his brothers and sisters again. When spring came, Service once more became restless, growing nostalgic for Dawson and his little cabin on the hillside.

Feeling exceptionally fit after the hard work of the farm, he chose to return to the Yukon via the Old Edmonton Trail, an arduous 2,000-mile route that had been touted as an all-Canada route to the Klondike. Despite a few harrowing experiences, Service found the trip delightful, and took copious notes with the intention of writing a book about it. The book never materialized, but the trek added to his reputation as the "Bard of the Yukon" and provided inspiration for many of the verses in his third book.

It was late summer 1911 when Service reached Dawson City, where he quickly resumed his old life. He spent the winter writing and by late spring *Rhymes of A Rolling Stone* was finished. Service was reluctant to quit Dawson, where he had been so happy; he finally left on the last boat of the year.

After leaving the Yukon, Service's books were generating enough income that he never again needed to worry about money.

He spent most of the remainder of his life in Europe. Longing for a change of scene, in 1912 he accepted an assignment to work as a war correspondent for the *Toronto Star* in the Balkans. The following year, he met and married Germaine Bourgoin in Paris; in 1917 they became parents of twin girls, Doris and Iris. A year later Doris caught scarlet fever and died. Service and his family divided their time between homes in Brittany, Paris and on the Riviera until 1940, when the outbreak of World War II forced them to flee to England. They then made their way to Montreal and finally Hollywood. There they made their home until December 1945, when they returned to France to live in Nice and spend summers in Brittany. Service died at Dream Haven, his beloved home on the Brittany coast, on September 11, 1958, with Germaine at his bedside.

In the end, Robert Service made his fortune with his words — in his lifetime he wrote six novels, two memoirs and more than 2,000 verses, allowing him to live in comfort and leave behind a trust fund for his granddaughters and an estate valued at $300,000. But of all that he wrote, he is still best known for the poems he wrote in the Yukon, which colorfully capture the essence of the Klondike Gold Rush. Today Service is commonly regarded as the most widely read poet of the 20th Century. ❧

— *Kathy Doogan*

A group from the Canadian Bank of Commerce, following
a dinner in Whitehorse celebrating publication of *Songs of
a Sourdough*, 1907. Robert Service is seated at back right.
(From *The Yukon*, Arthur Cherry Hinton, 1954)

1

Selected Poems from

Songs of a Sourdough (1907)

"It was a Saturday night, and from the various bars I
heard sounds of revelry. The line popped into my mind:
'A bunch of the boys were whooping it up,' and it stuck
there. Good enough for a start.... I was on fire to get
started.... [*The Shooting of Dan McGrew*] came so easily
to me in my excited state that I was amazed at my
facility. It was as if some one was whispering in my ear."

— Robert Service, in *Ploughman of the Moon,*
An Adventure Into Memory (1945)

Taking a breather between dances at Evaline's
Roadhouse, outside Dawson City, July 1903.
(Yukon Archives, Adams & Larkin Fonds, #9092)

The Shooting of Dan McGrew

A bunch of the boys were whooping it up in the Malamute saloon;
The kid that handles the music-box was hitting a jag-time tune;
Back of the bar, in a solo game, sat Dangerous Dan McGrew,
And watching his luck was his light-o'-love, the lady that's known as Lou.

When out of the night, which was fifty below, and into the din and the glare,
There stumbled a miner fresh from the creeks, dog-dirty, and loaded for bear.
He looked like a man with a foot in the grave and scarcely the strength of a louse,
Yet he tilted a poke of dust on the bar, and he called for drinks for the house.
There was none could place the stranger's face, though we searched ourselves for a clue;
But we drank his health, and the last to drink was Dangerous Dan McGrew.

There's men that somehow just grip your eyes, and hold them hard like a spell;
And such was he, and he looked to me like a man who had lived in hell;
With a face most hair, and the dreary stare of a dog whose day is done,
As he watered the green stuff in his glass, and the drops fell one by one.
Then I got to figgering who he was, and wondering what he'd do,
And I turned my head — and there watching him was the lady that's known as Lou.

His eyes went rubbering round the room, and he seemed in a kind of daze,
Till at last that old piano fell in the way of his wandering gaze.
The rag-time kid was having a drink; there was no one else on the stool,
So the stranger stumbles across the room, and flops down there like a fool.
In a buckskin shirt that was glazed with dirt he sat, and I saw him sway;
Then he clutched the keys with his talon hands — my God! but that man could play.

Were you ever out in the Great Alone, when the moon was awful clear,
And the icy mountains hemmed you in with a silence you most could HEAR;
With only the howl of a timber wolf, and you camped there in the cold,
A half-dead thing in a stark, dead world, clean mad for the muck called gold;
While high overhead, green, yellow and red, the North Lights swept in bars? —
Then you've a haunch what the music meant . . . hunger and night and the stars.

And hunger not of the belly kind, that's banished with bacon and beans,
But the gnawing hunger of lonely men for a home and all that it means;
For a fireside far from the cares that are, four walls and a roof above;
But oh! so cramful of cosy joy, and crowned with a woman's love —
A woman dearer than all the world, and true as Heaven is true —
(God! how ghastly she looks through her rouge, — the lady that's known as Lou.)

Then on a sudden the music changed, so soft that you scarce could hear;
But you felt that your life had been looted clean of all that it once held dear;
That someone had stolen the woman you loved; that her love was a devil's lie;
That your guts were gone, and the best for you was to crawl away and die.
'Twas the crowning cry of a heart's despair, and it thrilled you through and through —
"I guess I'll make it a spread misere," said Dangerous Dan McGrew.

The music almost died away . . . then it burst like a pent-up flood;
And it seemed to say, "Repay, repay," and my eyes were blind with blood.
The thought came back of an ancient wrong, and it stung like a frozen lash,
And the lust awoke to kill, to kill . . . then the music stopped with a crash,
And the stranger turned, and his eyes they burned in a most peculiar way;

In a buckskin shirt that was glazed with dirt he sat, and I saw him sway;
Then his lips went in in a kind of grin, and he spoke, and his voice was calm,
And "Boys," says he, "you don't know me, and none of you care a damn;
But I want to state, and my words are straight, and I'll bet my poke they're true,
That one of you is a hound of hell . . . and that one is Dan McGrew."

Then I ducked my head, and the lights went out, and two guns blazed in the dark,
And a woman screamed, and the lights went up, and two men lay stiff and stark.
Pitched on his head, and pumped full of lead, was Dangerous Dan McGrew,
While the man from the creeks lay clutched to the breast of the lady that's known as Lou.

These are the simple facts of the case, and I guess I ought to know.
They say that the stranger was crazed with "hooch," and I'm not denying it's so.
I'm not so wise as the lawyer guys, but strictly between us two —
The woman that kissed him and — pinched his poke — was the lady that's known as Lou.

A dance hall girl, around 1900.
(Glenbow Archives, NA-3439-1)

Miners near their sluice box, #5 From Mouth,
Gold Bottom Creek, around 1901. (Yukon
Archives, Adams & Larkin Fonds, #9091)

The Spell of the Yukon

I wanted the gold, and I sought it,
    I scrabbled and mucked like a slave.
Was it famine or scurvy — I fought it;
    I hurled my youth into a grave.
I wanted the gold, and I got it —
    Came out with a fortune last fall, —
Yet somehow life's not what I thought it,
    And somehow the gold isn't all.

No! There's the land. (Have you seen it?)
    It's the cussedest land that I know,
From the big, dizzy mountains that screen it
    To the deep, deathlike valleys below.
Some say God was tired when He made it;
    Some say it's a fine land to shun;
Maybe; but there's some as would trade it
    For no land on earth — and I'm one.

You come to get rich (damned good reason);
    You feel like an exile at first;
You hate it like hell for a season,
    And then you are worse than the worst.
It grips you like some kinds of sinning;
    It twists you from foe to a friend;
It seems it's been since the beginning;
    It seems it will be to the end.

I've stood in some mighty-mouthed hollow
    That's plumb-full of hush to the brim;
I've watched the big, husky sun wallow
    In crimson and gold, and grow dim,
Till the moon set the pearly peaks gleaming,
    And the stars tumbled out, neck and crop;
And I've thought that I surely was dreaming,
    With the peace o' the world piled on top.

The summer — no sweeter was ever;
    The sunshiny woods all athrill;
The grayling aleap in the river,
    The bighorn asleep on the hill.
The strong life that never knows harness;
    The wilds where the caribou call;
The freshness, the freedom, the farness —
    O God! how I'm stuck on it all.

The winter! the brightness that blinds you,
    The white land locked tight as a drum,
The cold fear that follows and finds you,
    The silence that bludgeons you dumb.
The snows that are older than history,
    The woods where the weird shadows slant;
The stillness, the moonlight, the mystery,
    I've bade 'em good-by — but I can't.

There's a land where the mountains are nameless,
    And the rivers all run God knows where;
There are lives that are erring and aimless,
    And deaths that just hang by a hair;
There are hardships that nobody reckons;
    There are valleys unpeopled and still;
There's a land — oh, it beckons and beckons,
    And I want to go back — and I will.

They're making my money diminish;
     I'm sick of the taste of champagne.
Thank God! when I'm skinned to a finish
     I'll pike to the Yukon again.
I'll fight — and you bet it's no sham-fight;
     It's hell! — but I've been there before;
And it's better than this by a damnsite —
     So me for the Yukon once more.

There's gold, and it's haunting and haunting;
     It's luring me on as of old;
Yet it isn't the gold that I'm wanting
     So much as just finding the gold.
It's the great, big, broad land 'way up yonder,
     It's the forests where silence has lease;
It's the beauty that thrills me with wonder,
     It's the stillness that fills me with peace.

Anna Eva Fay Pingree, famous magician, medium and mesmerist, 1899. Pingree performed in Dawson City in the late 1890s. (Glenbow Archives, NA-2883-65)

Clerks and customers in the money order department
of the Dawson Post Office, around 1901.
(Yukon Archives, Adams & Larkin Fonds, #9143)

The Law of the Yukon

This is the law of the Yukon, and ever she makes it plain:
"Send not your foolish and feeble; send me your strong and your sane —
Strong for the red rage of battle; sane for I harry them sore;
Send me men girt for the combat, men who are grit to the core;
Swift as the panther in triumph, fierce as the bear in defeat,
Sired of a bulldog parent, steeled in the furnace heat.
Send me the best of your breeding, lend me your chosen ones;
Them will I take to my bosom, them will I call my sons;
Them will I gild with my treasure, them will I glut with my meat;
But the others — the misfits, the failures — I trample under my feet.
Dissolute, damned and despairful, crippled and palsied and slain,
Ye would send me the spawn of your gutters — Go! take back your spawn again.

"Wild and wide are my borders, stern as death is my sway;
From my ruthless throne I have ruled alone for a million years and a day;
Hugging my mighty treasure, waiting for man to come,
Till he swept like a turbid torrent, and after him swept — the scum.
The pallid pimp of the dead-line, the enervate of the pen,
One by one I weeded them out, for all that I sought was — Men.
One by one I dismayed them, frighting them sore with my glooms;
One by one I betrayed them unto my manifold dooms.
Drowned them like rats in my rivers, starved them like curs on my plains,
Rotted the flesh that was left them, poisoned the blood in their veins;
Burst with my winter upon them, searing forever their sight,
Lashed them with fungus-white faces, whimpering wild in the night;

"Staggering blind through the storm-whirl, stumbling mad through the snow,
Frozen stiff in the ice-pack, brittle and bent like a bow;
Featureless, formless, forsaken, scented by wolves in their flight,
Left for the wind to make music through ribs that are glittering white;
Gnawing the black crust of failure, searching the pit of despair,
Crooking the toe in the trigger, trying to patter a prayer;
Going outside with an escort, raving with lips all afoam,
Writing a cheque for a million, driveling feebly of home;
Lost like a louse in the burning . . . or else in the tented town
Seeking a drunkard's solace, sinking and sinking down;
Steeped in the slime at the bottom, dead to a decent world,
Lost 'mid the human flotsam, far on the frontier hurled;
In the camp at the bend of the river, with its dozen saloons aglare,
Its gambling dens ariot, its gramophones all ablare;
Crimped with the crimes of a city, sin-ridden and bridled with lies,
In the hush of my mountained vastness, in the flush of my midnight skies.
Plague-spots, yet tools of my purpose, so natheless I suffer them thrive,
Crushing my Weak in their clutches, that only my Strong may survive.

"But the others, the men of my mettle, the men who would 'stablish my fame
Unto its ultimate issue, winning me honor, not shame;
Searching my uttermost valleys, fighting each step as they go,
Shooting the wrath of my rapids, scaling my ramparts of snow;
Ripping the guts of my mountains, looting the beds of my creeks,
Them will I take to my bosom, and speak as a mother speaks.
I am the land that listens, I am the land that broods;
Steeped in eternal beauty, crystalline waters and woods.
Long have I waited lonely, shunned as a thing accurst,
Monstrous, moody, pathetic, the last of the lands and the first;
Visioning camp-fires at twilight, sad with a longing forlorn,
Feeling my womb o'er-pregnant with the seed of cities unborn.
Wild and wide are my borders, stern as death is my sway,
And I wait for the men who will win me — and I will not be won in a day;
And I will not be won by weaklings, subtle, suave and mild,
But by men with the hearts of vikings, and the simple faith of a child;
Desperate, strong and resistless, unthrottled by fear or defeat,
Them will I gild with my treasure, them will I glut with my meat.

"Lofty I stand from each sister land, patient and wearily wise,
With the weight of a world of sadness in my quiet, passionless eyes;
Dreaming alone of a people, dreaming alone of a day,
When men shall not rape my riches, and curse me and go away;
Making a bawd of my bounty, fouling the hand that gave —
Till I rise in my wrath and I sweep on their path and I stamp them into a grave.
Dreaming of men who will bless me, of women esteeming me good,
Of children born in my borders of radiant motherhood,
Of cities leaping to stature, of fame like a flag unfurled,
As I pour the tide of my riches in the eager lap of the world."

This is the Law of the Yukon, that only the Strong shall thrive;
That surely the Weak shall perish, and only the Fit survive.
Dissolute, damned and despairful, crippled and palsied and slain,
This is the Will of the Yukon, — Lo, how she makes it plain!

Worker in mine shaft on #16 Eldorado Creek, about 1901.
(Yukon Archives, Adams & Larkin Fonds, #9089)

The Song of the Wage-Slave

When the long, long day is over, and the Big Boss gives me my pay,
I hope that it won't be hell-fire, as some of the parsons say.
And I hope that it won't be heaven, with some of the parsons I've met —
All I want is just quiet, just to rest and forget.
Look at my face, toil-furrowed; look at my calloused hands;
Master, I've done Thy bidding, wrought in Thy many lands —
Wrought for the little masters, big-bellied they be, and rich;
I've done their desire for a daily hire, and I die like a dog in a ditch.
I have used the strength Thou hast given, Thou knowest I did not shirk;
Threescore years of labor — Thine be the long day's work.
And now, Big Master, I'm broken and bent and twisted and scarred,
But I've held my job, and Thou knowest, and Thou will not judge me hard.
Thou knowest my sins are many, and often I've played the fool —
Whiskey and cards and women, they made me the devil's tool.
I was just like a child with money; I flung it away with a curse,
Feasting a fawning parasite, or glutting a harlot's purse;
Then back to the woods repentant, back to the mill or the mine,
I, the worker of workers, everything in my line.
Everything hard but headwork (I'd no more brains than a kid),
A brute with brute strength to labor, doing as I was bid;
Living in camps with men-folk, a lonely and loveless life;
Never knew kiss of sweetheart, never caress of wife.
A brute with brute strength to labor, and they were so far above —
Yet I'd gladly have gone to the gallows for one little look of Love.
I, with the strength of two men, savage and shy and wild —
Yet how I'd ha' treasured a woman, and the sweet, warm kiss of a child!
Well, 'tis Thy world, and Thou knowest. I blaspheme and my ways be rude;
But I've lived my life as I found it, and I've done my best to be good;
I, the primitive toiler, half naked and grimed to the eyes,
Sweating it deep in their ditches, swining it stark in their styes;
Hurling down forests before me, spanning tumultuous streams;
Down in the ditch building o'er me palaces fairer than dreams;

Boring the rock to the ore-bed, driving the road through the fen,
Resolute, dumb, uncomplaining, a man in a world of men.
Master, I've filled my contract, wrought in Thy many lands;
Not by my sins wilt Thou judge me, but by the work of my hands.
Master, I've done Thy bidding, and the light is low in the west,
And the long, long shift is over . . . Master, I've earned it — Rest.

Summit Blacksmith Shop at summit of the White Pass,
September 1898. (Yukon Archives, H.C. Barley Fonds, #5326)

Dawson City in winter, about 1906. Note sternwheelers
frozen in on the river. (Dawson City Museum &
Historical Society, 1984-72-1, R.C. Bower Collection)

The Cremation of Sam McGee

There are strange things done in the midnight sun
*   By the men who moil for gold;*
The Arctic trails have their secret tales
*   That would make your blood run cold;*
The Northern Lights have seen queer sights,
*   But the queerest they ever did see*
Was that night on the marge of Lake Lebarge
*   I cremated Sam McGee.*

Now Sam McGee was from Tennessee, where the cotton blooms and blows.
Why he left his home in the South to roam 'round the Pole, God only knows.
He was always cold, but the land of gold seemed to hold him like a spell;
Though he'd often say in his homely way that he'd "sooner live in hell."

On a Christmas Day we were mushing our way over the Dawson trail.
Talk of your cold! through the parka's fold it stabbed like a driven nail.
If our eyes we'd close, then the lashes froze till sometimes we couldn't see;
It wasn't much fun, but the only one to whimper was Sam McGee.

And that very night, as we lay packed tight in our robes beneath the snow,
And the dogs were fed, and the stars o'erhead were dancing heel and toe,
He turned to me, and "Cap," says he, "I'll cash in this trip, I guess;
And if I do, I'm asking that you won't refuse my last request."

Well, he seemed so low that I couldn't say no; then he says with a sort of moan:
"It's the cursed cold, and it's got right hold till I'm chilled clean through to the bone.
Yet 'tain't being dead — it's my awful dread of the icy grave that pains;
So I want you to swear that, foul or fair, you'll cremate my last remains."

A pal's last need is a thing to heed, so I swore I would not fail;
And we started on at the streak of dawn; but God! he looked ghastly pale.
He crouched on the sleigh, and he raved all day of his home in Tennessee;
And before nightfall a corpse was all that was left of Sam McGee.

There wasn't a breath in that land of death, and I hurried, horror-driven,
With a corpse half hid that I couldn't get rid, because of a promise given;
It was lashed to the sleigh, and it seemed to say: "You may tax your brawn and brains,
But you promised true, and it's up to you to cremate those last remains."

Now a promise made is a debt unpaid, and the trail has its own stern code.
In the days to come, though my lips were dumb, in my heart how I cursed that load.
In the long, long night, by the lone firelight, while the huskies, round in a ring,
Howled out their woes to the homeless snows — O God! how I loathed the thing.

And every day that quiet clay seemed to heavy and heavier grow;
And on I went, though the dogs were spent and the grub was getting low;
The trail was bad, and I felt half mad, but I swore I would not give in;
And I'd often sing to the hateful thing, and it hearkened with a grin.

Till I came to the marge of Lake Lebarge, and a derelict there lay;
It was jammed in the ice, but I saw in a trice it was called the "Alice May."
And I looked at it, and I thought a bit, and I looked at my frozen chum;
Then "Here," said I, with a sudden cry, "is my cre-ma-tor-eum."

Some planks I tore from the cabin floor, and I lit the boiler fire;
Some coal I found that was lying around, and I heaped the fuel higher;
The flames just soared, and the furnace roared — such a blaze you seldom see;
And I burrowed a hole in the glowing coal, and I stuffed in Sam McGee.

Then I made a hike, for I didn't like to hear him sizzle so;
And the heavens scowled, and the huskies howled, and the wind began to blow.
It was icy cold, but the hot sweat rolled down my cheeks, and I don't know why;
And the greasy smoke in an inky cloak went streaking down the sky.

I do not know how long in the snow I wrestled with grisly fear;
But the stars came out and they danced about ere again I ventured near;
I was sick with dread, but I bravely said: "I'll just take a peep inside.
I guess he's cooked, and it's time I looked;" . . . then the door I opened wide.

And there sat Sam, looking cool and calm, in the heart of the furnace roar;
And he wore a smile you could see a mile, and he said: "Please close that door.
It's fine in here, but I greatly fear you'll let in the cold and storm —
Since I left Plumtree, down in Tennessee, it's the first time I've been warm."

There are strange things done in the midnight sun
*   By the men who moil for gold;*
The Arctic trails have their secret tales
*   That would make your blood run cold;*
The Northern Lights have seen queer sights,
*   But the queerest they ever did see*
Was that night on the marge of Lake Lebarge
*   I cremated Sam McGee.*

Miners inside their cabin, Klondike gold fields, about
1901. (Yukon Archives, Adams & Larkin Fonds, #9140)

Popular Dawson City entertainer Cad Wilson at home,
late 1890s. (Dawson City Museum & Historical Society,
1994-259-57, Thora McIlroy Mills Collection)

My Madonna

I hailed me a woman from the street,
  Shameless, but, oh, so fair!
I bade her sit in the model's seat
  And I painted her sitting there.

I hid all trace of her heart unclean;
  I painted a babe at her breast;
I painted her as she might have been
  If the Worst had been the Best.

She laughed at my picture and went away.
  Then came, with a knowing nod,
A connoisseur, and I heard him say;
  "'Tis Mary, the Mother of God."

So I painted a halo round her hair,
  And I sold her and took my fee,
And she hangs in the church of Saint Hillaire,
  Where you and all may see.

Well-dressed men playing cards, early 1900s.
(Yukon Archives, H.C. Barley Fonds, #4746)

The Men That Don't Fit In

There's a race of men that don't fit in,
 A race that can't stay still;
So they break the hearts of kith and kin,
 And they roam the world at will.
They range the field and they rove the flood,
 And they climb the mountain's crest;
Theirs is the curse of the gypsy blood,
 And they don't know how to rest.

If they just went straight they might go far;
 They are strong and brave and true;
But they're always tired of the things that are,
 And they want the strange and new.
They say: "Could I find my proper groove,
 What a deep mark I would make!"
So they chop and change, and each fresh move
 Is only a fresh mistake.

And each forgets, as he strips and runs
 With a brilliant, fitful pace,
It's the steady, quiet, plodding ones
 Who win in the lifelong race.
And each forgets that his youth has fled,
 Forgets that his prime is past,
Till he stands one day, with a hope that's dead,
 In the glare of the truth at last.

He has failed, he has failed; he has missed his chance;
    He has just done things by half.
Life's been a jolly good joke on him,
    And now is the time to laugh.
Ha, ha! He is one of the Legion Lost;
    He was never meant to win;
He's a rolling stone, and it's bred in the bone;
    He's a man who won't fit in.

Interior view of lavishly decorated restaurant,
probably in Dawson City, about 1901.
(Yukon Archives, Adams & Larkin Fonds, #9146)

The Reckoning

It's fine to have a blow-out in a fancy restaurant,
With terrapin and canvas-back and all the wine you want;
To enjoy the flowers and music, watch the pretty women pass,
Smoke a choice cigar, and sip the wealthy water in your glass.
It's bully in a high-toned joint to eat and drink your fill,
But it's quite another matter when you
                    Pay the bill.

It's great to go out every night on fun or pleasure bent;
To wear your glad rags always and to never save a cent;
To drift along regardless, have a good time every trip;
To hit the high spots sometimes, and to let your chances slip;
To know you're acting foolish, yet to go on fooling still,
Till Nature calls a show-down, and you
                    Pay the bill.

Time has got a little bill — get wise while yet you may,
For the debit side's increasing in a most alarming way;
The things you had no right to do, the things you should have done,
They're all put down; it's up to you to pay for every one.
So eat, drink and be merry, have a good time if you will,
But God help you when the time comes, and you
                    Foot the bill.

Miners in front of log cabin, #5-15 Pup, Last
Chance Creek, about 1901. (Yukon Archives,
Adams & Larkin Fonds, #9156)

The Little Old Log Cabin

When a man gits on his uppers in a hard-pan sort of town,
    An' he ain't got nothin' comin' an' he can't afford ter eat,
An' he's in a fix for lodgin' an' he wanders up an' down,
    An' you'd fancy he'd been boozin', he's so locoed 'bout the feet;
When he's feelin' sneakin' sorry an' his belt is hangin' slack,
    An' his face is peaked an' gray-like an' his heart gits down an' whines,
Then he's apt ter git a-thinkin' an' a-wishin' he was back
    In the little ol' log cabin in the shadder of the pines.

When he's on the blazin' desert an' his canteen's sprung a leak,
    An' he's all alone an' crazy an' he's crawlin' like a snail,
An' his tongue's so black an' swollen that it hurts him fer to speak,
    An' he gouges down fer water an' the raven's on his trail;
When he's done with care and cursin' an' he feels more like to cry,
    An' he sees ol' Death a-grinnin' an' he thinks upon his crimes,
Then he's like ter hev' a vision, as he settles down ter die,
    Of the little ol' log cabin an' the roses an' the vines.

Oh, the little ol' log cabin, it's a solemn shinin' mark,
    When a feller gits ter sinnin' an' a-goin' ter the wall,
An' folks don't understand him an' he's gropin' in the dark,
    An' he's sick of bein' cursed at an' he's longin' fer his call!
When the sun of life's a-sinkin' you can see it 'way above,
    On the hill from out the shadder in a glory 'gin the sky,
An' your mother's voice is callin', an' her arms are stretched in love,
    An' somehow you're glad you're goin', an' you ain't a-scared to die;
When you'll be like a kid again an' nestle to her breast,
    An' never leave its shelter, an' forget, an' love, an' rest.

Robert Service in his canoe *Coquette* on the
Mackenzie River, Northwest Territories, 1911.
(Library and Archives Canada, PA-145189)

2

Selected Poems from

Ballads of a Cheechako (1909)

"In writing [*Ballads of a Cheechako*] I had to think more than I usually do. I don't like to have to think as I write. I prefer to sit down, and hope for the stuff to come.... But this time I really had to get down and dig. Instead of my usual joyous exuberance I blasted out my rhymes with grim determination. When I finished the last line my relief was enormous."

— Robert Service, in *Ploughman of the Moon, An Adventure Into Memory* (1945)

Sternwheelers tied up at Whitehorse, 1903.
(Yukon Archives, H.C. Barley Fonds, #5537)

Men of the High North

Men of the High North, the wild sky is blazing;
    Islands of opal float on silver seas;
Swift splendors kindle, barbaric, amazing;
    Pale ports of amber, golden argosies.
Ringed all around us the proud peaks are glowing;
    Fierce chiefs in council, their wigwam the sky;
Far, far below us the big Yukon flowing,
    Like threaded quicksilver, gleams to the eye.

Men of the High North, you who have known it;
    You in whose hearts its splendors have abode;
Can you renounce it, can you disown it?
    Can you forget it, its glory and its goad?
Where is the hardship, where is the pain of it?
    Lost in the limbo of things you've forgot;
Only remain the guerdon and gain of it;
    Zest of the foray, and God, how you fought!

You who have made good, you foreign faring;
    You money magic to far lands has whirled;
Can you forget those days of vast daring,
    There with your soul on the Top o' the World?
Nights when no peril could keep you awake on
    Spruce boughs you spread for your couch in the snow;
Taste all your feasts like the beans and the bacon
    Fried at the camp-fire at forty below?

Can you remember your huskies all going,
    Barking with joy and their brushes in air;
You in your parka, glad-eyed and glowing,
    Monarch, your subjects the wolf and the bear?
Monarch, your kingdom unravisht and gleaming;
    Mountains your throne, and a river your car;
Crash of a bull moose to rouse you from dreaming;
    Forest your couch, and your candle a star.

You who this faint day the High North is luring
 Unto her vastness, taintlessly sweet;
You who are steel-braced, straight-lipped, enduring,
 Dreadless in danger and dire in defeat:
Honor the High North ever and ever,
 Whether she crown you, or whether she slay;
Suffer her fury, cherish and love her —
 He who would rule he must learn to obey.

Men of the High North, fierce mountains love you;
 Proud rivers leap when you ride on their breast.
See, the austere sky, pensive above you,
 Dons all her jewels to smile on your rest.
Children of Freedom, scornful of frontiers,
 We who are weaklings honor your worth.
Lords of the wilderness, Princes of Pioneers,
 Let's have a rouse that will ring round the earth.

A hydraulic giant at a placer mining operation on
Victoria Gulch, 1914. (Dawson City Museum & Historical
Society, 1991-51-92, Vincent Vesco Collection)

Stampeders whipsawing lumber for boat building, Lake
Lindeman, 1899. (Yukon Archives, Anton Vogee Fonds, #133)

A dog team at work in front of Eldorado Bottling
and Steam Laundry Co., Dawson City, summer 1899.
(Yukon Archives, H.C. Barley Fonds, #4712)

The Ballad of Blasphemous Bill

I took a contract to bury the body of blasphemous Bill MacKie,
Whenever, wherever or whatsoever the manner of death he die —
Whether he die in the light o' day or under the peak-faced moon;
In cabin or dance-hall, camp or dive, mucklucks or patent shoon;
On velvet tundra or virgin peak, by glacier, drift or draw;
In muskeg hollow or canyon gloom, by avalanche, fang or claw;
By battle, murder or sudden wealth, by pestilence, hooch or lead —
I swore on the Book I would follow and look till I found my tombless dead.

For Bill was a dainty kind of cuss, and his mind was mighty sot
On a dinky patch with flowers and grass in a civilized bone-yard lot.
And where he died or how he died, it didn't matter a damn
So long as he had a grave with frills and a tombstone "epigram."
So I promised him, and he paid the price in good cheechako coin
(Which the same I blowed in that very night down in the Tenderloin).
Then I painted a three-foot slab of pine: "Here lies poor Bill MacKie,"
And I hung it up on my cabin wall and I waited for Bill to die.

Years passed away, and at last one day came a squaw with a story strange,
Of a long-deserted line of traps 'way back of the Bighorn range;
Of a little hut by the great divide, and a white man stiff and still,
Lying there by his lonesome self, and I figured it must be Bill.
So I thought of the contract I'd made with him, and I took down from the shelf
The swell black box with the silver plate he'd picked out for hisself;
And I packed it full of grub and "hooch," and I slung it on the sleigh;
Then I harnessed up my team of dogs and was off at dawn of day.

You know what it's like in the Yukon wild when it's sixty-nine below;
When the ice-worms wriggle their purple heads through the crust of the pale blue snow;
When the pine-trees crack like little guns in the silence of the wood,
And the icicles hang down like tusks under the parka hood;
When the stove-pipe smoke breaks sudden off, and the sky is weirdly lit,
And the careless feel of a bit of steel burns like a red-hot spit;
When the mercury is a frozen ball, and the frost-fiend stalks to kill —
Well, it was just like that that day when I set out to look for Bill.

Oh, the awful hush that seemed to crush me down on every hand,
As I blundered blind with a trail to find through that blank and bitter land;
Half dazed, half crazed in the winter wild, with its grim heart-breaking woes,
And the ruthless strife for a grip on life that only the sourdough knows!
North by the compass, North I pressed; river and peak and plain
Passed like a dream I slept to lose and I waked to dream again.

Miners with a mastodon tusk and moose antlers, Dawson City,
July 1899. (Yukon Archives, H.C. Barley Fonds, #4714)

River and plain and mighty peak — and who could stand unawed?
As their summits blazed, he could stand undazed at the foot of the throne of God.
North, aye, North, through a land accurst, shunned by the scouring brutes,
And all I heard was my own harsh word and the whine of the malamutes,
Till at last I came to a cabin squat, built in the side of a hill,
And I burst in the door, and there on the floor, frozen to death, lay Bill.

Ice, white ice, like a winding-sheet, sheathing each smoke-grimed wall;
Ice on the stove-pipe, ice on the bed, ice gleaming over all;
Sparkling ice on the dead man's chest, glittering ice in his hair,
Ice on his fingers, ice in his heart, ice in his glassy stare;
Hard as a log and trussed like a frog, with his arms and legs outspread.
I gazed at the coffin I'd brought for him, and I gazed at the gruesome dead,
And at last I spoke: "Bill liked his joke; but still, goldarn his eyes,
A man had ought to consider his mates in the way he goes and dies."

Have you ever stood in an Arctic hut in the shadow of the Pole,
With a little coffin six by three and a grief you can't control?
Have you ever sat by a frozen corpse that looks at you with a grin,
And that seems to say: "You may try all day, but you'll never jam me in"?
I'm not a man of the quitting kind, but I never felt so blue
As I sat there gazing at that stiff and studying what I'd do.
Then I rose and I kicked off the husky dogs that were nosing round about,
And I lit a roaring fire in the stove, and I started to thaw Bill out.

Well, I thawed and thawed for thirteen days, but it didn't seem no good;
His arms and legs stuck out like pegs, as if they was made of wood.
Till at last I said: "It ain't no use — he's froze too hard to thaw;
He's obstinate, and he won't lie straight, so I guess I got to — saw."
So I sawed off poor Bill's arms and legs, and I laid him snug and straight
In the little coffin he picked hisself, with the dinky silver plate;
And I came nigh near to shedding a tear as I nailed him safely down;
Then I stowed him away in my Yukon sleigh, and I started back to town.

So I buried him as the contract was in a narrow grave and deep,
And there he's waiting the Great Clean-up, when the Judgment sluice-heads sweep;
And I smoke my pipe and I meditate in the light of the Midnight Sun,
And sometimes I wonder if they was, the awful things I done.
And as I sit and the parson talks, expounding of the Law,
I often think of poor old Bill — and how hard he was to saw.

Panorama of Dawson City from the hills behind town,
July 1903. (Yukon Archives, H.C. Barley Fonds, #4703)

The Ballad of One-Eyed Mike

This is the tale that was told to me by the man with the crystal eye,
As I smoked my pipe in the camp-fire light, and the Glories swept the sky;
As the Northlights gleamed and curved and streamed, and the bottle of "hooch" was dry.

A man once aimed that my life be shamed, and wrought me a deathly wrong;
I vowed one day I would well repay, but the heft of his hate was strong.
He thonged me East and he thonged me West; he harried me back and forth,
Till I fled in fright from his peerless spite to the bleak, bald-headed North.

And there I lay, and for many a day I hatched plan after plan,
For a golden haul of the wherewithal to crush and to kill my man;
And there I strove, and there I clove through the drift of icy streams;
And there I fought, and there I sought for the pay-streak of my dreams.

So twenty years, with their hopes and fears and smiles and tears and such,
Went by and left me long bereft of hope of the Midas touch;
About as fat as a chancel rat, and lo! despite my will,
In the weary fight I had clean lost sight of the man I sought to kill.

'Twas so far away, that evil day when I prayed to the Prince of Gloom
For the savage strength and the sullen length of life to work his doom.
Nor sign nor word had I seen or heard, and it happed so long ago;
My youth was gone and my memory wan, and I willed it even so.

It fell one night in the waning light by the Yukon's oily flow,
I smoked and sat as I marvelled at the sky's port-winey glow;
Till it paled away to an absinthe gray, and the river seemed to shrink,
All wobbly flakes and wriggling snakes and goblin eyes a-wink.

'Twas weird to see and it 'wildered me in a queer, hypnotic dream,
Till I saw a spot like an inky blot come floating down the stream;
It bobbed and swung; it sheered and hung; it romped round in a ring;
It seemed to play in a tricksome way; it sure was a merry thing.

In freakish flights strange oily lights came fluttering round its head,
Like butterflies of a monster size — then I knew it for the Dead.
Its face was rubbed and slicked and scrubbed as smooth as a shaven pate;
In the silver snakes that the water makes it gleamed like a dinner-plate.

It gurgled near, and clear and clear and large and large it grew;
It stood upright in a ring of light and it looked me through and through.
It weltered round with a woozy sound, and ere I could retreat,
With the witless roll of a sodden soul it wantoned to my feet.

And here I swear by this Cross I wear, I heard that "floater" say:
"I am the man from whom you ran, the man you sought to slay.
That you may note and gaze and gloat, and say `Revenge is sweet',
In the grit and grime of the river's slime I am rotting at your feet.

"The ill we rue we must e'en undo, though it rive us bone from bone;
So it came about that I sought you out, for I prayed I might atone.
I did you wrong, and for long and long I sought where you might live;
And now you're found, though I'm dead and drowned, I beg you to forgive."

So sad it seemed, and its cheek-bones gleamed, and its fingers flicked the shore;
And it lapped and lay in a weary way, and its hands met to implore;
That I gently said: "Poor, restless dead, I would never work you woe;
Though the wrong you rue you can ne'er undo, I forgave you long ago."

Then, wonder-wise, I rubbed my eyes and I woke from a horrid dream.
The moon rode high in the naked sky, and something bobbed in the stream.
It held my sight in a patch of light, and then it sheered from the shore;
It dipped and sank by a hollow bank, and I never saw it more.

This was the tale he told to me, that man so warped and gray,
Ere he slept and dreamed, and the camp-fire gleamed in his eye in a wolfish way —
That crystal eye that raked the sky in the weird Auroral ray.

Stampeders and their pack dogs, early 1900s.
(Yukon Archives, H.C. Barley Fonds, #5133)

Interior of the North-West Mounted
Police guardroom, Whitehorse, 1915.
(Glenbow Archives, NA-1663-21)

My Friends

The man above was a murderer, the man below was a thief;
And I lay there in the bunk between, ailing beyond belief;
A weary armful of skin and bone, wasted with pain and grief.

My feet were froze, and the lifeless toes were purple and green and gray;
The little flesh that clung to my bones, you could punch it in holes like clay;
The skin on my gums was a sullen black, and slowly peeling away.

I was sure enough in a direful fix, and often I wondered why
They did not take the chance that was left and leave me alone to die,
Or finish me off with a dose of dope — so utterly lost was I.

But no; they brewed me the green-spruce tea, and nursed me there like a child;
And the homicide he was good to me, and bathed my sores and smiled;
And the thief he starved that I might be fed, and his eyes were kind and mild.

Yet they were woefully wicked men, and often at night in pain
I heard the murderer speak of his deed and dream it over again;
I heard the poor thief sorrowing for the dead self he had slain.

I'll never forget that bitter dawn, so evil, askew and gray,
When they wrapped me round in the skins of beasts and they bore me to a sleigh,
And we started out with the nearest post an hundred miles away.

I'll never forget the trail they broke, with its tense, unuttered woe;
And the crunch, crunch, crunch as their snowshoes sank through the crust of the hollow snow;
And my breath would fail, and every beat of my heart was like a blow.

And oftentimes I would die the death, yet wake up to life anew;
The sun would be all ablaze on the waste, and the sky a blighting blue,
And the tears would rise in my snow-blind eyes and furrow my cheeks like dew.

And the camps we made when their strength outplayed and the day was pinched and wan;
And oh, the joy of that blessed halt, and how I did dread the dawn;
And how I hated the weary men who rose and dragged me on.

And oh, how I begged to rest, to rest — the snow was so sweet a shroud;
And oh, how I cried when they urged me on, cried and cursed them aloud;
Yet on they strained, all racked and pained, and sorely their backs were bowed.

And then it was all like a lurid dream, and I prayed for a swift release
From the ruthless ones who would not leave me to die alone in peace;
Till I wakened up and I found myself at the post of the Mounted Police.

And there was my friend the murderer, and there was my friend the thief,
With bracelets of steel around their wrists, and wicked beyond belief:
But when they come to God's judgment seat — may I be allowed the brief.

The Canadian Bank of Commerce, Front Street, Dawson
City, 1900. (Yukon Archives, Anton Vogee Fonds, #77)

The Ballad of Hard-Luck Henry

Now wouldn't you expect to find a man an awful crank
That's staked out nigh three hundred claims, and every one a blank;
That's followed every fool stampede, and seen the rise and fall
Of camps where men got gold in chunks and he got none at all;
That's prospected a bit of ground and sold it for a song
To see it yield a fortune to some fool that came along;
That's sunk a dozen bed-rock holes, and not a speck in sight,
Yet sees them take a million from the claims to left and right?
Now aren't things like that enough to drive a man to booze?
But Hard-Luck Smith was hoodoo-proof — he knew the way to lose.

'Twas in the fall of nineteen four — leap-year I've heard them say —
When Hard-Luck came to Hunker Creek and took a hillside lay.
And lo! as if to make amends for all the futile past,
Late in the year he struck it rich, the real pay-streak at last.
The riffles of his sluicing-box were choked with speckled earth,
And night and day he worked that lay for all that he was worth.
And when in chill December's gloom his lucky lease expired,
He found that he had made a stake as big as he desired.

One day while meditating on the waywardness of fate,
He felt the ache of lonely man to find a fitting mate;
A petticoated pard to cheer his solitary life,
A woman with soft, soothing ways, a confidant, a wife.
And while he cooked his supper on his little Yukon stove,
He wished that he had staked a claim in Love's rich treasure-trove;
When suddenly he paused and held aloft a Yukon egg,
For there in pencilled letters was the magic name of Peg.

You know these Yukon eggs of ours — some pink, some green, some blue —
A dollar per, assorted tints, assorted flavors too.
The supercilious cheechako might designate them high,
But one acquires a taste for them and likes them by-and-by.
Well, Hard-Luck Henry took this egg and held it to the light,
And there was more faint pencilling that sorely taxed his sight.
At last he made it out, and then the legend ran like this —
"Will Klondike miner write to Peg, Plumhollow, Squashville, Wis.?"

That night he got to thinking of this far-off, unknown fair;
It seemed so sort of opportune, an answer to his prayer.
She flitted sweetly through his dreams, she haunted him by day,
She smiled through clouds of nicotine, she cheered his weary way.
At last he yielded to the spell; his course of love he set —
Wisconsin his objective point; his object, Margaret.

With every mile of sea and land his longing grew and grew.
He practised all his pretty words, and these, I fear, were few.
At last, one frosty evening, with a cold chill down his spine,
He found himself before her house, the threshold of the shrine.
His courage flickered to a spark, then glowed with sudden flame —
He knocked; he heard a welcome word; she came — his goddess came.
Oh, she was fair as any flower, and huskily he spoke:
"I'm all the way from Klondike, with a mighty heavy poke.
I'm looking for a lassie, one whose Christian name is Peg,
Who sought a Klondike miner, and who wrote it on an egg."

The lassie gazed at him a space, her cheeks grew rosy red;
She gazed at him with tear-bright eyes, then tenderly she said:
"Yes, lonely Klondike miner, it is true my name is Peg.
It's also true I longed for you and wrote it on an egg.
My heart went out to someone in that land of night and cold;
But oh, I fear that Yukon egg must have been mighty old.
I waited long, I hoped and feared; you should have come before;
I've been a wedded woman now for eighteen months or more.
I'm sorry, since you've come so far, you ain't the one that wins;
But won't you take a step inside — *I'll let you see the twins.*"

School children and teachers in front of their schoolhouse,
about 1901. (Yukon Archives, Adams & Larkin Fonds, #9082)

The Yukon's largest gold dredge at work in the Klondike River Valley, July 1913. (Dawson City Museum & Historical Society, 1991-51-68, Vincent Vesco Collection)

The Prospector

I strolled up old Bonanza, where I staked in ninety-eight,
    A-purpose to revisit the old claim.
I kept thinking mighty sadly of the funny ways of Fate,
    And the lads who once were with me in the game.
Poor boys, they're down-and-outers, and there's scarcely one to-day
    Can show a dozen colors in his poke;
And me, I'm still prospecting, old and battered, gaunt and gray,
    And I'm looking for a grub-stake, and I'm broke.

I strolled up old Bonanza. The same old moon looked down;
    The same old landmarks seemed to yearn to me;
But the cabins all were silent, and the flat, once like a town,
    Was mighty still and lonesome-like to see.
There were piles and piles of tailings where we toiled with pick and pan,
    And turning round a bend I heard a roar,
And there a giant gold-ship of the very newest plan
    Was tearing chunks of pay-dirt from the shore.

It wallowed in its water-bed; it burrowed, heaved and swung;
    It gnawed its way ahead with grunts and sighs;
Its bill of fare was rock and sand; the tailings were its dung;
    It glared around with fierce electric eyes.
Full fifty buckets crammed its maw; it bellowed out for more;
    It looked like some great monster in the gloom.
With two to feed its sateless greed, it worked for seven score,
    And I sighed: "Ah, old-time miner, here's your doom!"

The idle windlass turns to rust; the sagging sluice-box falls;
    The holes you digged are water to the brim;
Your little sod-roofed cabins with the snugly moss-chinked walls
    Are deathly now and mouldering and dim.
The battle-field is silent where of old you fought it out;
    The claims you fiercely won are lost and sold;
But there's a little army that they'll never put to rout —
    The men who simply live to seek the gold.

The men who can't remember when they learned to swing a pack,
    Or in what lawless land the quest began;
The solitary seeker with his grub-stake on his back,
    The restless buccaneer of pick and pan.
On the mesas of the Southland, on the tundras of the North,
    You will find us, changed in face but still the same;
And it isn't need, it isn't greed that sends us faring forth —
    It's the fever, it's the glory of the game.

For once you've panned the speckled sand and seen the bonny dust,
    Its peerless brightness blinds you like a spell;
It's little else you care about; you go because you must,
    And you feel that you could follow it to hell.
You'd follow it in hunger, and you'd follow it in cold;
    You'd follow it in solitude and pain;
And when you're stiff and battened down let someone whisper "Gold,"
    You're lief to rise and follow it again.

Yet look you, if I find the stuff it's just like so much dirt;
    I fling it to the four winds like a child.
It's wine and painted women and the things that do me hurt,
    Till I crawl back, beggared, broken, to the Wild.
Till I crawl back, sapped and sodden, to my grub-stake and my tent —
    There's a city, there's an army (hear them shout).
There's the gold in millions, millions, but I haven't got a cent;
    And oh, it's me, it's me that found it out.

It was my dream that made it good, my dream that made me go
    To lands of dread and death disprized of man;
But oh, I've known a glory that their hearts will never know,
    When I picked the first big nugget from my pan.
It's still my dream, my dauntless dream, that drives me forth once more
    To seek and starve and suffer in the Vast;
That heaps my heart with eager hope, that glimmers on before —
    My dream that will uplift me to the last.

Perhaps I am stark crazy, but there's none of you too sane;
　　It's just a little matter of degree.
My hobby is to hunt out gold; it's fortressed in my brain;
　　It's life and love and wife and home to me.
And I'll strike it, yes, I'll strike it; I've a hunch I cannot fail;
　　I've a vision, I've a prompting, I've a call;
I hear the hoarse stampeding of an army on my trail,
　　To the last, the greatest gold camp of them all.

Beyond the shark-tooth ranges sawing savage at the sky
　　There's a lowering land no white man ever struck;
There's gold, there's gold in millions, and I'll find it if I die,
　　And I'm going there once more to try my luck.
Maybe I'll fail — what matter? It's a mandate, it's a vow;
　　And when in lands of dreariness and dread
You seek the last lone frontier, far beyond your frontiers now,
　　You will find the old prospector, silent, dead.

You will find a tattered tent-pole with a ragged robe below it;
You will find a rusted gold-pan on the sod;
You will find the claim I'm seeking, with my bones as stakes to show it;
But I've sought the last Recorder, and He's — God.

A prospector with a rocker box and gold pan, Klondike
gold fields, 1908. (Dawson City Museum & Historical
Society, 1991-51-21, Vincent Vesco Collection)

Stampeder's outfits cached on Chilkoot Pass, 1898.
(E.A. Hegg, Library & Archives Canada, C-28672)

The Trail of Ninety-Eight

I.

Gold! We leapt from our benches. Gold! We sprang from our stools.
Gold! We wheeled in the furrow, fired with the faith of fools.
Fearless, unfound, unfitted, far from the night and the cold,
Heard we the clarion summons, followed the master-lure — Gold!

Men from the sands of the Sunland; men from the woods of the West;
Men from the farms and the cities, into the Northland we pressed.
Graybeards and striplings and women, good men and bad men and bold,
Leaving our homes and our loved ones, crying exultantly — "Gold!"

Never was seen such an army, pitiful, futile, unfit;
Never was seen such a spirit, manifold courage and grit.
Never has been such a cohort under one banner unrolled
As surged to the ragged-edged Arctic, urged by the arch-tempter — Gold.

"Farewell!" we cried to our dearests; little we cared for their tears.
"Farewell!" we cried to the humdrum and the yoke of the hireling years;
Just like a pack of school-boys, and the big crowd cheered us good-bye.
Never were hearts so uplifted, never were hopes so high.

The spectral shores flitted past us, and every whirl of the screw
Hurled us nearer to fortune, and ever we planned what we'd do —
Do with the gold when we got it — big, shiny nuggets like plums,
There in the sand of the river, gouging it out with our thumbs.

And one man wanted a castle, another a racing stud;
A third would cruise in a palace yacht like a red-necked prince of blood.
And so we dreamed and we vaunted, millionaires to a man,
Leaping to wealth in our visions long ere the trail began.

II.

We landed in wind-swept Skagway. We joined the weltering mass,
Clamoring over their outfits, waiting to climb the Pass.
We tightened our girths and our pack-straps; we linked on the Human Chain,
Struggling up to the summit, where every step was a pain.

Gone was the joy of our faces, grim and haggard and pale;
The heedless mirth of the shipboard was changed to the care of the trail.
We flung ourselves in the struggle, packing our grub in relays,
Step by step to the summit in the bale of the winter days.

Floundering deep in the sump-holes, stumbling out again;
Crying with cold and weakness, crazy with fear and pain.
Then from the depths of our travail, ere our spirits were broke,
Grim, tenacious and savage, the lust of the trail awoke.

"Klondike or bust!" rang the slogan; every man for his own.
Oh, how we flogged the horses, staggering skin and bone!
Oh, how we cursed their weakness, anguish they could not tell,
Breaking their hearts in our passion, lashing them on till they fell!

For grub meant gold to our thinking, and all that could walk must pack;
The sheep for the shambles stumbled, each with a load on its back;
And even the swine were burdened, and grunted and squealed and rolled,
And men went mad in the moment, huskily clamoring "Gold!"

Oh, we were brutes and devils, goaded by lust and fear!
Our eyes were strained to the summit; the weaklings dropped to the rear,
Falling in heaps by the trail-side, heart-broken, limp and wan;
But the gaps closed up in an instant, and heedless the chain went on.

Never will I forget it, there on the mountain face,
Antlike, men with their burdens, clinging in icy space;
Dogged, determined and dauntless, cruel and callous and cold,
Cursing, blaspheming, reviling, and ever that battle-cry — "Gold!"

Thus toiled we, the army of fortune, in hunger and hope and despair,
Till glacier, mountain and forest vanished, and, radiantly fair,
There at our feet lay Lake Bennett, and down to its welcome we ran:
The trail of the land was over, the trail of the water began.

III.

We built our boats and we launched them. Never has been such a fleet;
A packing-case for a bottom, a mackinaw for a sheet.
Shapeless, grotesque, lopsided, flimsy, makeshift and crude,
Each man after his fashion builded as best he could.

Each man worked like a demon, as prow to rudder we raced;
The winds of the Wild cried "Hurry!" the voice of the waters, "Haste!"
We hated those driving before us; we dreaded those pressing behind;
We cursed the slow current that bore us; we prayed to the God of the wind.

Spring! and the hillsides flourished, vivid in jewelled green;
Spring! and our hearts' blood nourished envy and hatred and spleen.
Little cared we for the Spring-birth; much cared we to get on —
Stake in the Great White Channel, stake ere the best be gone.

The greed of the gold possessed us; pity and love were forgot;
Covetous visions obsessed us; brother with brother fought.
Partner with partner wrangled, each one claiming his due;
Wrangled and halved their outfits, sawing their boats in two.

Thuswise we voyaged Lake Bennett, Tagish, then Windy Arm,
Sinister, savage and baleful, boding us hate and harm.
Many a scow was shattered there on that iron shore;
Many a heart was broken straining at sweep and oar.

A pack train carrying turkeys, en route to Dawson
City, 1898. (Glenbow Archives, NA-3602-1)

We roused Lake Marsh with a chorus, we drifted many a mile;
There was the canyon before us — cave-like its dark defile;
The shores swept faster and faster; the river narrowed to wrath;
Waters that hissed disaster reared upright in our path.

Beneath us the green tumult churning, above us the cavernous gloom;
Around us, swift twisting and turning, the black, sullen walls of a tomb.
We spun like a chip in a mill-race; our hearts hammered under the test;
Then — oh, the relief on each chill face! — we soared into sunlight and rest.

Hand sought for hand on the instant. Cried we, "Our troubles are o'er!"
Then, like a rumble of thunder, heard we a canorous roar.
Leaping and boiling and seething, saw we a cauldron afume;
There was the rage of the rapids, there was the menace of doom.

The river springs like a racer, sweeps through a gash in the rock;
Buts at the boulder-ribbed bottom, staggers and rears at the shock;
Leaps like a terrified monster, writhes in its fury and pain;
Then with the crash of a demon springs to the onset again.

Dared we that ravening terror; heard we its din in our ears;
Called on the Gods of our fathers, juggled forlorn with our fears;
Sank to our waists in its fury, tossed to the sky like a fleece;
Then, when our dread was the greatest, crashed into safety and peace.

But what of the others that followed, losing their boats by the score?
Well could we see them and hear them, strung down that desolate shore.
What of the poor souls that perished? Little of them shall be said —
On to the Golden Valley, pause not to bury the dead.

Then there were days of drifting, breezes soft as a sigh;
Night trailed her robe of jewels over the floor of the sky.
The moonlit stream was a python, silver, sinuous, vast,
That writhed on a shroud of velvet — well, it was done at last.

There were the tents of Dawson, there the scar of the slide;
Swiftly we poled o'er the shallows, swiftly leapt o'er the side.
Fires fringed the mouth of Bonanza; sunset gilded the dome;
The test of the trail was over — thank God, thank God, we were Home!

North-West Mounted Police at Chico, along the
Whitehorse-Dawson Trail near Lake Laberge, 1900.
(Yukon Archives, H.C. Barley Fonds, #4921)

Robert Service in his cabin in Dawson City, around 1911.
(Yukon Archives, Gillis Family Fonds, #4535)

3

Selected Poems from

Rhymes of a Rolling Stone (1912)

"So all that winter I worked at [*Rhymes of a Rolling
Stone*]; not too hard nor too anxiously, for I had lots
of time and knew it would come out all right. My first
book had been written with no thought of publication;
my second was a *tour de force* produced in the small
hours of the morning; but this one was a leisured and
pleasant job spread over most of a year."

— Robert Service, in *Ploughman of the Moon,
An Adventure Into Memory* (1945)

A picnic party at Lake Bennett, August 1899.
(Yukon Archives, H.C. Barley Fonds, #4799)

The Land of Beyond

Have ever you heard of the Land of Beyond,
    That dreams at the gates of the day?
Alluring it lies at the skirts of the skies,
    And ever so far away;
Alluring it calls: O ye the yoke galls,
    And ye of the trail overfond,
With saddle and pack, by paddle and track,
    Let's go to the Land of Beyond!

Have ever you stood where the silences brood,
    And vast the horizons begin,
At the dawn of the day to behold far away
    The goal you would strive for and win?
Yet ah! in the night when you gain to the height,
    With the vast pool of heaven star-spawned,
Afar and agleam, like a valley of dream,
    Still mocks you a Land of Beyond.

Thank God! there is always a Land of Beyond
    For us who are true to the trail;
A vision to seek, a beckoning peak,
    A farness that never will fail;
A pride in our soul that mocks at a goal,
    A manhood that irks at a bond,
And try how we will, unattainable still,
    Behold it, our Land of Beyond!

Sternwheelers *Whitehorse*, *Dawson* and *Selkirk* after construction was
completed at British-Yukon Navigation Co.'s shipyard, Whitehorse,
May 25, 1901. (Yukon Archives, H.C. Barley Fonds, #5550)

Athabaska Dick

When the boys come out from Lac Labiche in the lure of the early Spring,
To take the pay of the "Hudson's Bay," as their fathers did before,
They are all a-glee for the jamboree, and they make the Landing ring
With a whoop and a whirl, and a "Grab your girl," and a rip and a skip and a roar.
For the spree of Spring is a sacred thing, and the boys must have their fun;
Packer and tracker and half-breed Cree, from the boat to the bar they leap;
And then when the long flotilla goes, and the last of their pay is done,
The boys from the banks of Lac Labiche swing to the heavy sweep.
And oh, how they sigh! and their throats are dry, and sorry are they and sick:
Yet there's none so cursed with a lime-kiln thirst as that Athabaska Dick.

He was long and slim and lean of limb, but strong as a stripling bear;
And by the right of his skill and might he guided the Long Brigade.
All water-wise were his laughing eyes, and he steered with a careless care,
And he shunned the shock of foam and rock, till they came to the Big Cascade.
And here they must make the long portage, and the boys sweat in the sun;
And they heft and pack, and they haul and track, and each must do his trick;
But their thoughts are far in the Landing bar, where the founts of nectar run:
And no man thinks of such gorgeous drinks as that Athabaska Dick.

'Twas the close of day and his long boat lay just over the Big Cascade,
When there came to him one Jack-pot Jim, with a wild light in his eye;
And he softly laughed, and he led Dick aft, all eager, yet half afraid,
And snugly stowed in his coat he showed a pilfered flask of "rye."
And in haste he slipped, or in fear he tripped, but — Dick in warning roared —
And there rang a yell, and it befell that Jim was overboard.

Oh, I heard a splash, and quick as a flash I knew he could not swim.
I saw him whirl in the river swirl, and thresh his arms about.
In a queer, strained way I heard Dick say: "I'm going after him,"
Throw off his coat, leap down the boat — and then I gave a shout:
"Boys, grab him, quick! You're crazy, Dick! Far better one than two!
Hell, man! You know you've got no show! It's sure and certain death. . . ."
And there we hung, and there we clung, with beef and brawn and thew,
And sinews cracked and joints were racked, and panting came our breath;
And there we swayed and there we prayed, till strength and hope were spent —
Then Dick, he threw us off like rats, and after Jim he went.

With mighty urge amid the surge of river-rage he leapt,
And gripped his mate and desperate he fought to gain the shore;
With teeth a-gleam he bucked the stream, yet swift and sure he swept
To meet the mighty cataract that waited all a-roar.
And there we stood like carven wood, our faces sickly white,
And watched him as he beat the foam, and inch by inch he lost;
And nearer, nearer drew the fall, and fiercer grew the fight,
Till on the very cascade crest a last farewell he tossed.
Then down and down and down they plunged into that pit of dread;
And mad we tore along the shore to claim our bitter dead.

And from that hell of frenzied foam, that crashed and fumed and boiled,
Two little bodies bubbled up, and they were heedless then;
And oh, they lay like senseless clay! and bitter hard we toiled,
Yet never, never gleam of hope, and we were weary men.
And moments mounted into hours, and black was our despair;
And faint were we, and we were fain to give them up as dead,
When suddenly I thrilled with hope: "Back, boys! and give him air;
I feel the flutter of his heart. . . ." And, as the word I said,
Dick gave a sigh, and gazed around, and saw our breathless band;
And saw the sky's blue floor above, all strewn with golden fleece;
And saw his comrade Jack-pot Jim, and touched him with his hand:
And then there came into his eyes a look of perfect peace.
And as there, at his very feet, the thwarted river raved,
I heard him murmur low and deep:
                    "Thank God! the whiskey's saved."

Party-goers after a Fourth of July dance at Skagway,
July 1899. (Yukon Archives, H.C. Barley Fonds, #5070)

A woodcutter on the White Pass & Yukon
Route Railway construction crew, September 1898.
(Yukon Archives, H.C. Barley Fonds, #5335)

The Quitter

When you're lost in the Wild, and you're scared as a child,
    And Death looks you bang in the eye,
And you're sore as a boil, it's according to Hoyle
    To cock your revolver and . . . die.
But the Code of a Man says: "Fight all you can,"
    And self-dissolution is barred.
In hunger and woe, oh, it's easy to blow . . .
    It's the hell-served-for-breakfast that's hard.

"You're sick of the game!" Well, now, that's a shame.
    You're young and you're brave and you're bright.
"You've had a raw deal!" I know — but don't squeal,
    Buck up, do your damnedest, and fight.
It's the plugging away that will win you the day,
    So don't be a piker, old pard!
Just draw on your grit; it's so easy to quit:
    It's the keeping-your-chin-up that's hard.

It's easy to cry that you're beaten — and die;
    It's easy to crawfish and crawl;
But to fight and to fight when hope's out of sight —
    Why, that's the best game of them all!
And though you come out of each gruelling bout,
    All broken and beaten and scarred,
Just have one more try — it's dead easy to die,
    It's the keeping-on-living that's hard.

Two customers in the Hub Saloon, Dawson City.
(E.O. Ellingsen, Library & Archives Canada, C-018650)

The Cow Juice Cure

The clover was in blossom, an' the year was at the June,
When Flap-jack Billy hit the town, likewise O'Flynn's saloon.
The frost was on the fodder an' the wind was growin' keen,
When Billy got to seein' snakes in Sullivan's shebeen.

Then in meandered Deep-hole Dan, once comrade of the cup:
"Oh Billy, for the love of Mike, why don't ye sober up?
I've got the gorgus recipay, 'tis smooth an' slick as silk —
Jest quit yer strangle-holt on hooch, an' irrigate with milk.
Lackteal flooid is the lubrication you require;
Yer nervus frame-up's like a bunch of snarled piano wire.
You want to get it coated up with addypose tishoo,
So's it will work elastic-like, an' milk's the dope for you."

Well, Billy was complyable, an' in a month it's strange,
That cow-juice seemed to oppyrate a most amazin' change.
"Call up the water-wagon, Dan, an' book my seat," sez he.
"'Tis mighty queer," sez Deep-hole Dan, "'twas just the same with me."
They shanghaied little Tim O'Shane, they cached him safe away,
An' though he objurgated some, they "cured" him night an' day;
An' pretty soon there came the change amazin' to explain:
"I'll never take another drink," sez Timothy O'Shane.
They tried it out on Spike Muldoon, that toper of renown;
They put it over Grouch McGraw, the terror of the town.
They roped in "tanks" from far and near, an' every test was sure,
An' like a flame there ran the fame of Deep-hole's Cow-juice Cure.

"It's mighty queer," sez Deep-hole Dan, "I'm puzzled through and through;
It's only milk from Riley's ranch, no other milk will do."
An' it jest happened on that night with no predictive plan,
He left some milk from Riley's ranch a-settin' in a pan;
An' picture his amazement when he poured that milk next day —
There in the bottom of the pan a dozen "colours" lay.

"Well, what d'ye know 'bout that," sez Dan; "Gosh ding my dasted eyes,
We've been an' had the Gold Cure, Bill, an' none of us was wise.
The milk's free-millin' that's a cinch; there's colours everywhere.
Now, let us figger this thing out — how does the dust git there?
`Gold from the grass-roots down', they say — why, Bill! we've got it cold —
Them cows what nibbles up the grass, jest nibbles up the gold.
We're blasted, bloomin' millionaires; dissemble an' lie low:
We'll follow them gold-bearin' cows, an' prospect where they go."

An' so it came to pass, fer weeks them miners might be found
A-sneakin' round on Riley's ranch, an' snipin' at the ground;
Till even Riley stops an' stares, an' presently allows:
"Them boys appear to take a mighty interest in cows."
An' night an' day they shadowed each auriferous bovine,
An' panned the grass-roots on their trail, yet nivver gold they seen.
An' all that season, secret-like, they worked an' nothin' found;
An' there was colours in the milk, but none was in the ground.
An' mighty desperate was they, an' down upon their luck,
When sudden, inspirationlike, the source of it they struck.
An' where d'ye think they traced it to? it grieves my heart to tell —
In the black sand at the bottom of that wicked milkman's *well*.

A meat market on Third Avenue, Dawson City, 1900.
(Yukon Archives, H.C. Barley Fonds, #4710)

Miners with a freshly-baked loaf of bread in their
camp near Teslin Lake, June 1898. (H.J. Woodside,
Library and Archives Canada, PA-016141)

While the Bannock Bakes

Light up your pipe again, old chum, and sit awhile with me;
I've got to watch the bannock bake — how restful is the air!
You'd little think that we were somewhere north of Sixty-three,
Though where I don't exactly know, and don't precisely care.
The man-size mountains palisade us round on every side;
The river is a-flop with fish, and ripples silver-clear;
The midnight sunshine brims yon cleft — we think it's the Divide;
We'll get there in a month, maybe, or maybe in a year.

It doesn't matter, does it, pal? We're of that breed of men
With whom the world of wine and cards and women disagree;
Your trouble was a roofless game of poker now and then,
And "raising up my elbow," that's what got away with me.
We're merely "Undesirables," artistic more or less;
My horny hands are Chopin-wise; you quote your Browning well;
And yet we're fooling round for gold in this damned wilderness:
The joke is, if we found it, we would both go straight to hell.

Well, maybe we won't find it — and at least we've got the "life."
We're both as brown as berries, and could wrestle with a bear:
(That bannock's raising nicely, pal; just jab it with your knife.)
Fine specimens of manhood they would reckon us out there.
It's the tracking and the packing and the poling in the sun;
It's the sleeping in the open, it's the rugged, unfaked food;
It's the snow-shoe and the paddle, and the campfire and the gun,
And when I think of what I was, I know that it is good.

Just think of how we've poled all day up this strange little stream;
Since life began no eye of man has seen this place before;
How fearless all the wild things are! the banks with goose-grass gleam,
And there's a bronzy musk-rat sitting sniffing at his door.
A mother duck with brood of ten comes squattering along;
The tawny, white-winged ptarmigan are flying all about;
And in that swirly, golden pool, a restless, gleaming throng,
The trout are waiting till we condescend to take them out.

Ah, yes, it's good! I'll bet that there's no doctor like the Wild:
(Just turn that bannock over there; it's getting nicely brown.)
I might be in my grave by now, forgotten and reviled,
Or rotting like a sickly cur in some far, foreign town.
I might be that vile thing I was, — it all seems like a dream;
I owed a man a grudge one time that only life could pay;
And yet it's half-forgotten now — how petty these things seem!
(But that's "another story," pal; I'll tell it you some day.)

How strange two "irresponsibles" should chum away up here!
But round the Arctic Circle friends are few and far between.
We've shared the same camp-fire and tent for nigh on seven year,
And never had a word that wasn't cheering and serene.
We've halved the toil and split the spoil, and borne each other's packs;
By all the Wild's freemasonry we're brothers, tried and true;
We've swept on danger side by side, and fought it back to back,
And you would die for me, old pal, and I would die for you.

Now there was that time I got lost in Rory Bory Land,
(How quick the blizzards sweep on one across that Polar sea!)
You formed a rescue crew of One, and saw a frozen hand
That stuck out of a drift of snow — and, partner, it was Me.
But I got even, did I not, that day the paddle broke?
White water on the Coppermine — a rock — a split canoe —
Two fellows struggling in the foam (one couldn't swim a stroke):
A half-drowned man I dragged ashore . . . and partner, it was You.

In Rory Borealis Land the winter's long and black.
The silence seems a solid thing, shot through with wolfish woe;
And rowelled by the eager stars the skies vault vastly back,
And man seems but a little mite on that weird-lit plateau.
No thing to do but smoke and yarn of wild and misspent lives,
Beside the camp-fire there we sat — what tales you told to me
Of love and hate, and chance and fate, and temporary wives!
In Rory Borealis Land, beside the Arctic Sea.

One yarn you told me in those days I can remember still;
It seemed as if I visioned it, so sharp you sketched it in;
Bellona was the name, I think; a coast town in Brazil,
Where nobody did anything but serenade and sin.
I saw it all — the jewelled sea, the golden scythe of sand,
The stately pillars of the palms, the feathery bamboo,
The red-roofed houses and the swart, sun-dominated land,
The people ever children, and the heavens ever blue.

You told me of that girl of yours, that blossom of old Spain,
All glamour, grace and witchery, all passion, verve and glow.
How maddening she must have been! You made me see her plain,
There by our little camp-fire, in the silence and the snow.
You loved her and she loved you. She'd a husband, too, I think,
A doctor chap, you told me, whom she treated like a dog,
A white man living on the beach, a hopeless slave to drink —
(Just turn that bannock over there, that's propped against the log.)

That story seemed to strike me, pal — it happens every day:
You had to go away awhile, then somehow it befell
The doctor chap discovered, gave her up, and disappeared;
You came back, tired of her in time . . . there's nothing more to tell.
Hist! see those willows silvering where swamp and river meet!
Just reach me up my rifle quick; that's Mister Moose, I know —
There now, *I've got him dead to rights* . . . but hell! we've lots to eat
I don't believe in taking life — we'll let the beggar go.

Heigh ho! I'm tired; the bannock's cooked; it's time we both turned in.
The morning mist is coral-kissed, the morning sky is gold.
The camp-fire's a confessional — what funny yarns we spin!
It sort of made me think a bit, that story that you told.
The fig-leaf belt and Rory Bory are such odd extremes,
Yet after all how very small this old world seems to be...
Yes, that was quite a yarn, old pal, and yet to me it seems
You missed the point: the point is that the "doctor chap"...was ME...

A studio portrait of Gertrude MacFarlane, a nurse in
Dawson City, 1905. (Dawson City Museum & Historical
Society, 1994-259-10, Thora McIlroy Mills Collection)

The Wanderlust

The Wanderlust has lured me to the seven lonely seas,
Has dumped me on the tailing-piles of dearth;
The Wanderlust has haled me from the morris chairs of ease,
Has hurled me to the ends of all the earth.
How bitterly I've cursed it, oh, the Painted Desert knows,
The wraithlike heights that hug the pallid plain,
The all-but-fluid silence, — yet the longing grows and grows,
And I've got to glut the Wanderlust again.

      Soldier, sailor, in what a plight I've been!
      Tinker, tailor, oh what a sight I've seen!
      And I'm hitting the trail in the morning, boys,
      And you won't see my heels for dust;
      For it's "all day" with you
      When you answer the cue
            Of the Wan-der-lust.

The Wanderlust has got me . . . by the belly-aching fire,
By the fever and the freezing and the pain;
By the darkness that just drowns you, by the wail of home desire,
I've tried to break the spell of it — in vain.
Life might have been a feast for me, now there are only crumbs;
In rags and tatters, beggar-wise I sit;
Yet there's no rest or peace for me, imperious it drums,
The Wanderlust, and I must follow it.

      Highway, by-way, many a mile I've done;
      Rare way, fair way, many a height I've won;
      But I'm pulling my freight in the morning, boys,
      And it's over the hills or bust;
      For there's never a cure
      When you list to the lure
            Of the Wan-der-lust.

The Wanderlust has taught me . . . it has whispered to my heart
Things all you stay-at-homes will never know.
The white man and the savage are but three short days apart,
Three days of cursing, crawling, doubt and woe.
Then it's down to chewing muclucs, to the water you can eat,
To fish you bolt with nose held in your hand.
When you get right down to cases, it's King's Grub that rules the races,
And the Wanderlust will help you understand.

    Haunting, taunting, that is the spell of it;
    Mocking, baulking, that is the hell of it;
    But I'll shoulder my pack in the morning, boys,
    And I'm going because I must;
    For it's so-long to all
    When you answer the call
            Of the Wan-der-lust.

The Wanderlust has blest me . . . in a ragged blanket curled,
I've watched the gulf of Heaven foam with stars;
I've walked with eyes wide open to the wonder of the world,
I've seen God's flood of glory burst its bars.
I've seen the gold a-blinding in the riffles of the sky,
Till I fancied me a bloated plutocrat;
But I'm freedom's happy bond-slave, and I will be till I die,
And I've got to thank the Wanderlust for that.

    Wild heart, child heart, all of the world your home.
    Glad heart, mad heart, what can you do but roam?
    Oh, I'll beat it once more in the morning, boys,
    With a pinch of tea and a crust;
    For you cannot deny
    When you hark to the cry
            Of the Wan-der-lust.

The Wanderlust will claim me at the finish for its own.
I'll turn my back on men and face the Pole.
Beyond the Arctic outposts I will venture all alone;
Some Never-never Land will be my goal.
Thank God! there's none will miss me, for I've been a bird of flight;
And in my moccasins I'll take my call;
For the Wanderlust has ruled me,
And the Wanderlust has schooled me,
And I'm ready for the darkest trail of all.

　　Grim land, dim land, oh, how the vastness calls!
　　Far land, star land, oh, how the stillness falls!
　　For you never can tell if it's heaven or hell,
　　And I'm taking the trail on trust;
　　But I haven't a doubt
　　That my soul will leap out
　　　　On its Wan-der-lust.

The Dawsons vs. the Victorias, Dawson City,
April 13, 1904. (Glenbow Archives, NA-2883-31)

Interior of the Alaska Exploration Co.'s
department store, Dawson City, about 1901.
(Yukon Archives, Adams & Larkin Fonds, #9070)

The Baldness of Chewed-Ear

When Chewed-ear Jenkins got hitched up to Guinneyveer McGee,
His flowin' locks, ye recollect, wuz frivolous an' free;
But in old Hymen's jack-pot, it's a most amazin' thing,
Them flowin' locks jest disappeared like snow-balls in the Spring;
Jest seemed to wilt an' fade away like dead leaves in the Fall,
An' left old Chewed-ear balder than a white-washed cannon ball.

Now Missis Chewed-ear Jenkins, that wuz Guinneyveer McGee,
Wuz jest about as fine a draw as ever made a pair;
But when the boys got joshin' an' suggested it was she
That must be inflooenshul for the old man's slump in hair —
Why! Missis Chewed-ear Jenkins jest went clean up in the air.

"To demonstrate," sez she that night, "the lovin' wife I am,
I've bought a dozen bottles of Bink's Anty-Dandruff Balm.
'Twill make yer hair jest sprout an' curl like squash-vines in the sun,
An' I'm propose to sling it on till every drop is done."
That hit old Chewed-ear's funny side, so he lays back an' hollers:
"The day you raise a hair, old girl, you'll git a thousand dollars."

Now, whether 'twas the prize or not 'tis mighty hard to say,
But Chewed-ear didn't seem to have much comfort from that day.
With bottles of that dandruff dope she followed at his heels,
An' sprinkled an' massaged him even when he ate his meals.
She waked him from his beauty sleep with tender, lovin' care,
An' rubbed an' scrubbed assiduous, yet never sign of hair.

Well, naturally all the boys soon tumbled to the joke,
An' at the Wow-wow's Social 'twas Cold-deck Davis spoke:
"The little woman's working mighty hard on Chewed-ear's crown;
Let's give her for a three-fifth's share a hundred dollars down.
We stand to make five hundred clear — boys, drink in whiskey straight:
'The Chewed-ear Jenkins Hirsute Propagation Syndicate'."

The boys wuz on, an' soon chipped in the necessary dust;
They primed up a committy to negotiate the deal;
Then Missis Jenkins yielded, bein' rather in disgust,
An' all wuz signed an' witnessed, an' invested with a seal.
They rounded up old Chewed-ear, an' they broke it what they'd done;
Allowed they'd bought an interest in his chance of raisin' hair;
They yanked his hat off anxiouslike, opinin' one by one
Their magnifyin' glasses showed fine prospects everywhere.
They bought Hairlene, an' Thatchem, an' Jay's Capillery Juice,
An' Seven Something Sisters, an' Macassar an' Bay Rum,
An' everyone insisted on his speshul right to sluice
His speshul line of lotion onto Chewed-ear's cranium.
They only got the merrier the more the old man roared,
An' shares in "Jenkins Hirsute" went sky-highin' on the board.

The Syndicate wuz hopeful that they'd demonstrate the pay,
An' Missis Jenkins laboured in her perseverin' way.
The boys discussed on "surface rights," an' "out-crops" an' so on,
An' planned to have it "crown" surveyed, an' blue prints of it drawn.
They ran a base line, sluiced an' yelled, an' everyone wuz glad,
Except the balance of the property, an' he wuz "mad."
"It gives me pain," he interjects, "to squash yer glowin' dream,
But you wuz fools when you got in on this here 'Hirsute' scheme.
You'll never raise a hair on me," when lo! that very night,
Preparin' to retire he got a most onpleasant fright:
For on that shinin' dome of his, so prominently bare,
He felt the baby outcrop of a second growth of hair.

A thousand dollars! Sufferin' Caesar! Well, it must be saved!
He grabbed his razor recklesslike, an' shaved an' shaved an' shaved.
An' when his head was smooth again he gives a mighty sigh,
An' sneaks away, an' buys some Hair Destroyer on the sly.
So there wuz Missis Jenkins with "Restorer" wagin' fight,
An' Chewed-ear with "Destroyer" circumventin' her at night.
The battle wuz a mighty one; his nerves wuz on the strain,
An' yet in spite of all he did that hair began to gain.

The situation grew intense, so quietly one day,
He gave his share-holders the slip, an' made his get-a-way.
Jest like a criminal he skipped, an' aimed to defalcate
The Chewed-ear Jenkins Hirsute Propagation Syndicate.
His guilty secret burned him, an' he sought the city's din:
"I've got to get a wig," sez he, "to cover up my sin.
It's growin', growin' night an' day; it's most amazin' hair;"
An' when he looked at it that night, he shuddered with despair.
He shuddered an' suppressed a cry at what his optics seen —
For on my word of honour, boys, that hair wuz growin' *green*.

At first he guessed he'd get some dye, an' try to dye it black;
An' then he saw 'twas Nemmysis wuz layin' on his track.
He must jest face the music, an' confess the thing he done,
An' pay the boys an' Guinneyveer the money they had won.
An' then there came a big idee — it thrilled him like a shock:
Why not control the Syndicate by buyin' up the Stock?

An' so next day he hurried back with smoothly shaven pate,
An' for a hundred dollars he bought up the Syndicate.
'Twas mighty frenzied finance an' the boys set up a roar,
But "Hirsutes" from the market wuz withdrawn for evermore.
An' to this day in Nuggetsville they tell the tale how slick
The Syndicate sold out too soon, and Chewed-ear turned the trick.

North-West Mounted Police Constable A.E. Acland
chopping a tree on the Dalton Trail, June 1899.
(Yukon Archives, H.C. Barley Fonds, #4685)

A Song of Success

Ho! we were strong, we were swift, we were brave.
Youth was a challenge, and Life was a fight.
All that was best in us gladly we gave,
Sprang from the rally, and leapt for the height.
Smiling is Love in a foam of Spring flowers:
Harden our hearts to him — on let us press!
Oh, what a triumph and pride shall be ours!
See where it beacons, the star of success!

Cares seem to crowd on us — so much to do;
New fields to conquer, and time's on the wing.
Grey hairs are showing, a wrinkle or two;
Somehow our footstep is losing its spring.
Pleasure's forsaken us, Love ceased to smile;
Youth has been funeralled; Age travels fast.
Sometimes we wonder: is it worth while?
There! we have gained to the summit at last.

Aye, we have triumphed! Now must we haste,
Revel in victory . . . why! what is wrong?
Life's choicest vintage is flat to the taste —
Are we too late? Have we laboured too long?
Wealth, power, fame we hold . . . ah! but the truth:
Would we not give this vain glory of ours
For one mad, glad year of glorious youth,
Life in the Springtide, and Love in the flowers.

St. Mary's Hospital (left) and Catholic
church, Dawson City, summer 1901.
(Yukon Archives, H.C. Barley Fonds, #4715)

Heart O' the North

And when I come to the dim trail-end,
    I who have been Life's rover,
This is all I would ask, my friend,
    Over and over and over:

A little space on a stony hill
    With never another near me,
Sky o' the North that's vast and still,
    With a single star to cheer me;

Star that gleams on a moss-grey stone
    Graven by those who love me —
There would I lie alone, alone,
    With a single pine above me;

Pine that the north wind whinneys through —
    Oh, I have been Life's lover!
But there I'd lie and listen to
    Eternity passing over.

Additional Reading

Poetry Collections:

Songs of a Sourdough. Toronto: William Briggs, 1907. London: Fisher Unwin, 1907

The Spell of the Yukon. New York: Barse and Hopkins, 1907. Philadelphia: E. Stern and Co., 1907.

Ballads of a Cheechako. Toronto: William Briggs, 1909. New York: Barse and Hopkins, 1909. Philadelphia: E. Stern and Co., 1909.

Rhymes of a Rolling Stone. Toronto: William Briggs, 1912. New York: Dodd Mead, 1912. London: Fisher Unwin, 1913.

Memoirs:

Ploughman of the Moon, An Adventure Into Memory. New York: Dodd Mead, 1945. London: Ernest Benn, 1946.

Harper of Heaven, A Record of Radiant Living. New York: Dodd Mead, 1948. London: Ernest Benn, 1948.

Biographies:

Robert Service, A Biography. Carl F. Klink, McGraw Hill Ryerson, 1976.

On the Trail of Robert Service. G. Wallace Lockhart, Lauth Press, Baar, Girvan, 1991. Revised 1998.

Vagabond of Verse. James Mackay, Mainstream Publishing, 1995.

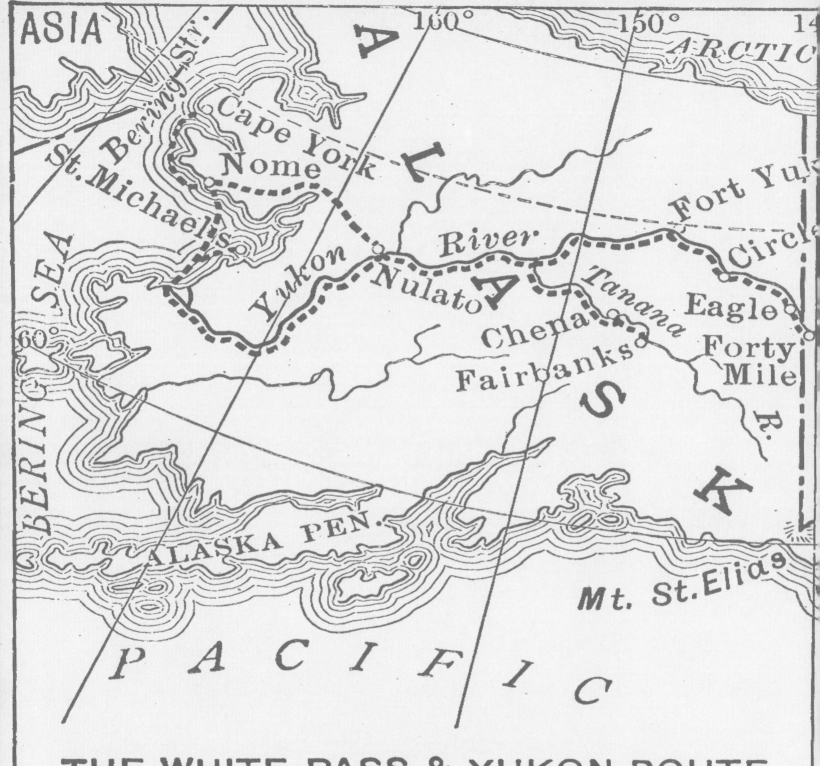

THE WHITE PASS & YUKON ROUTE
VIA SKAGUAY IS
The Gateway to the Golden North
The Land of Nightless Days